Wonders of the Rainforest

STEPHEN BLYTHE

DEDICATION

This book is dedicated to the teachers around the world who are teaching our children about the wonders of rainforests – and of nature in general – because it is only through a keen appreciation of the wonders of nature that we will work to protect and preserve our planet.

ACKNOWLEDGEMENTS

Cover photograph is by Bjørn Christian Tørrissen – another intrepid explorer and lover of the rainforests - with his very kind permission. I would also like to thank Michael Blythe for his editing assistance. All photographs in this book, except where otherwise noted, are by the author.

Stephen Blythe

Welcome to the Rainforest!

Rainforests are large forests which get a lot of rain allowing the plants to grow quickly. They usually have dense plant life supporting a large variety of animal life as well.

There are both temperate rainforests and tropical rainforests. Although we mostly think about tropical rainforests, and that is the subject of this book, we should not forget that there are a few areas of the world with cooler temperate rainforests that are also special wild places.

The picture to the right is from British Columbia, Canada. That is an old-growth red cedar tree below which I pitched my tent. It was as awesome as any tropical rainforest tree I have ever seen!

Tropical rainforests are characterized by being very hot and very wet! Sometimes this makes them unpleasant places to visit, but the rewards are plenty! Large tropical rainforests such as the Amazon even generate much of their own weather. In the Amazon massive quantities of water move from the ground up the roots and through the trees to the leaves where it evaporates (a process called transpiration). This moisture rises and cools, creating clouds, which frequently then produce rain.

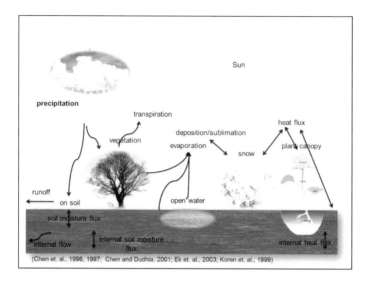

This NASA photograph shows the mouth of the Amazon where it drains into the Atlantic Ocean. You can see the formation of clouds only over the jungle – a result of transpiration.

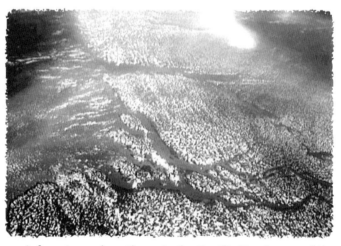

Other rainforests, such as those in the Pacific Northwest of North America and throughout Central America, benefit from having a constant flow of moist air coming off the nearby ocean which produces abundant rainfall.

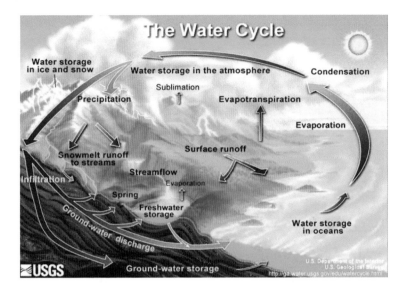

The forests of the world are critically important to us as they contain most of the earth's plants that convert carbon dioxide into the oxygen all animals breathe and which helps to maintain the planet's temperature and rain cycles. The tropical rainforests of the earth are home to half of the species of life on the planet - a single large tree in the Amazon may be home to over 100 different species of ants. The Amazon River and its tributaries have over 1,100 species of fish. We have learned that within this amazing variety of plants and animals are ones that can benefit mankind as sources of new medicines. We are beginning to see that preservation of these forests is vitally important to our future well-being on this planet!

The Tropical Rainforest Structure

Tropical rainforests are divided into four layers. There is the forest canopy, the understory, the forest floor, and the emergent layer.

The **_rainforest canopy_** is made of the tops of the trees which have reached open sky and spread out to collect sunlight. The canopy is defined by sunlight – plants that need sunlight must compete to grow to the canopy – or in some cases they actually start growing already in the canopy or halfway there.

You can see the canopy up close on this canopy walkway at the Amazon Center for Education and Research in Peru.

Trees must compete to grow tall to reach the sunlight of the canopy. Rather than send down deep roots for support, some tropical rainforest trees use other methods to support their height while growing quickly. Some trees have buttress roots – sort of like wings that grow sideways from the base of the tree to prevent it from falling sideways because of the shallow root structure.

The buttress roots on this tree, which was about a mile from the river's edge, also demonstrate the high-water mark where the Amazon River floods each year – this dark line was about ten feet above the ground. In the Amazon, the plants and animals have not only adapted to the tropical rainforest climate, they have adapted to surviving four months of each year with floodwaters!

Another method of support is prop roots, which grow sideways from the lower trunk to "prop up" the tree.

Imagine a tree that not only has prop roots but which can move if it isn't getting enough sunlight!

The locals call this the "walking tree." It sends more prop roots down in the direction of the sun and reabsorbs ones on the shady side and over a period of years the tree can actually reposition itself (by a little bit).

Not all plants that need sunlight have to start on the forest floor. Tropical rainforest canopies are filled with "epiphytes" – Latin for "upon plants." These are plants that grow on the bark of trees and get their nutrients from rainwater and the decaying bark of the trees. The most common epiphytes are bromeliads and orchids. There are also terrestrial (ground-based) types of both of these plants.

This photo is a blooming bromeliad growing on the side of a tree which was in a clearing.

Vines have adapted to "hitch-hike" on the tall growth of trees.

Vines can grow quickly to the canopy without the requirement for support, since they attach themselves to trees. Tropical rainforests are filled with vines.

These vines can make passage through the jungle extremely difficult in places.

The most aggressive vine anywhere is the "strangler fig" which starts growing part of the way up a tree when the seed lands in a little moist niche. The seed sends a branch upwards towards the canopy while it sends a root downwards to the soil. If the root successfully reaches the ground, the vine grows quickly, completely covering the host tree. Eventually the vine becomes larger than the host tree, killing it. The result looks not like a vine but more like a tree.

In this photo the strangler fig can be seen growing upwards to the left of the palm tree it is growing upon, and its roots have embraced the trunk of the tree and will eventually strangle it.

This strangler fig has completely enveloped the host tree, which can be seen poking out from within the "trunk" of the strangler. In another few years this tree will die and the strangler will become a "tree" of its own.

The canopy is where you will find the majority of the flowers and fruits of the rainforest. This is where many of the animals that eat nectar and fruit will be found – as well as the animals that eat them!

This squirrel monkey searches the canopy for fruit. Many monkeys are omnivores and will eat bird eggs, insects, and crustaceans such as crabs when they find them.

Monkeys are especially adapted to live in the rainforest canopy – most are small and nimble, and have opposable thumbs just like humans, which enables them to grab onto small branches as they leap from tree to tree. They are able to cover a large territory to find ripening fruit.

Although we think of monkeys as small, nimble, and friendly, there are exceptions. Baboons and chimps can be quite aggressive. In Borneo, there is a monkey called a proboscis monkey (because of the very large nose of the males). In spite of the large size reached by these monkeys, they can still jump from tree to tree – sometimes causing the whole tree to bend under their weight.

I spotted this huge proboscis monkey - the size of an 8-year old child - jumping through the treetops at Bako National Park in Borneo.

In the Amazon, the pygmy marmoset – the smallest of all monkeys – has a unique source of food. They make small holes through the outer bark of certain trees, then return to eat the sugary sap that weeps from the holes.

In Manuel Antonio National Park in Costa Rica the white-faced capuchin monkeys are brazen enough to steal your food if you leave it out, but generally eat everything from fruit to bird's eggs to crabs.

Other mammals also take to the canopy. This coati is foraging for fruit and eggs in the treetops, but is just as happy on the ground looking for food.

The **understory** of the rainforest is the area below the canopy. Except near the shores of a river, lake, or pond, the understory is very hot and humid and the air is still. In the understory you will find all the plants trying to grow up to the canopy and some low-growing plants, often in a clearing in a small patch of sunlight. The understory is the freeway between the forest floor and the canopy, and many animals – birds, mammals, insects, and reptiles commute between the floor and canopy in search of food.

Many creatures live in the understory – there are many hiding places, and lots of smaller creatures to eat! Butterflies, bugs, hummingbirds, bats – and many, many types of each. In Costa Rica, for example, there are 250 species of mammals – **half** of which are bats.

In the darkness of the Amazon understory I turned around and saw a shaft of light, and there in the light was this giant 10-inch torch ginger flower — an amazing sight.

And this little toad was sitting on a nearby leaf in the Amazon understory.

On the **forest floor** lives insects and bugs of all types, snakes, and those mammals that can't climb trees. The floor of the rainforest is a thin layer of decaying vegetation. The soil is shallow, so tree roots don't go very far down.

The moisture and shadows promotes the growth of mushrooms and other fungi that speed up the cycle of breakdown and regeneration.

An agouti, above, is a little rodent that scurries about the forest floor looking for things to eat. A frog comes out at night to sing for a mate. The forest floor can be a busy place!

The palm viper hunts at night for food on the forest floor, then curls up on a nearby branch to sleep the day away. Snakes are even eerie when they sleep – without eyelids, their eyes stay open, and you don't know if they are sleeping or just watching!

The palm viper is one of the most poisonous snakes in the Amazon. I was told that you may have two hours to live if you get bit. Considering that we were at least a one hour hike and then five hours by speedboat away from the nearest clinic, I asked my guide what they do when someone gets bit. "We take you to the shaman," he said. I didn't ask about the shaman's success rate! Note: when trekking through the Amazon Rainforest it is always wise to wear your knee-high thick rubber boots – not only because of the muddy spots but because they will offer some protection against snake bites.

At the Explorama Lodge in the Amazon, a tapir that has become accustomed to getting some left-overs helps himself into the dining room after the guests have finished their dinner:

In the Amazon, the water is not only home to many unique species of fish (such as the piranha), but also to unique water plants, the most famous being the giant water lilies:

When you consider that the number of different species of insects in the Amazon may be 20 to 30 million (there are over 7,000 species of butterflies alone), it is not surprising that you can be surprised by the strange variety of insects.

I was surprised by this wax-tailed leaf-hopper when I looked down and saw it. It is definitely one of the most amazing insects ever.

The *emergent layer* of the rainforest consists of trees that are growing taller than surrounding trees, sticking up above the canopy. They offer nesting and roosting spots for birds and monkeys. Their tall advantage may eventually result in a newer, taller canopy of new trees.

Adaptation for Survival

It has been estimated that the Amazon Rainforest is as much as 100 million years old. With the vast size and age this has allowed the huge number of different species to adapt to survive in unique ways. Adaptation allows an animal to have an advantage by decreasing its chances of being eaten and increasing its chances of finding something to eat!

Camouflage

One of the most common adaptations for survival is camouflage – being able to blend in to the background so as not to be seen by predators and to allow getting close to your own prey. One good example is the vine snake:

The vine snake curls up around a branch, looking like a vine, and goes unnoticed until something to eat comes along.

Many animals have adapted coloration and even patterns that allow them to blend in to the background. This large Agrippa moth may go unnoticed by a passing bird:

 And these six tiny long-nosed bats sleep the day away on a mottled branch sticking out of the Tahuayo River:

At night this nightjar rests on the forest floor – neatly blending in:

And what better camouflage than to be invisible! The glass wing butterfly has adapted to blend in to its environment by being transparent:

This iguana, although he enjoys basking in the sun, would be easy pickings for a passing hawk if he were not nearly invisible against the backdrop of the rock he is sitting upon:

And this lizard blends in with the log upon which he is sitting, waiting for a tasty bug to come along:

Can you spot the toad sitting in the leaves on the forest floor in this picture? He has found his niche:

And a green beetle can only hang out on a green leaf!

This frog has camouflage – that looks like it could have been the model for military camouflage! The mottled color makes it harder for predators to see his outline.

And this mantis matches his background:

Now you see it...Now you don't!

The most brilliant of all of the butterflies in the world is unquestionably the Blue Morpho. You would think that any insect this big and bright would be easy prey.

BUT – you will NEVER see a Blue Morpho exposing his blue upper wings when he is sitting still (the butterfly in this photo is a dead one at a museum!).

The undersides of the Blue Morpho' s wings are a mottled dull brown design which evolved to look like a dead leaf or to blend in with the forest floor. And when it flies, you see fluttering flashes of brilliant blue followed by nothing (as he closes his wings) and then a few feet away more flashes of brilliant blue. If you ever try to follow the flight of a Blue Morpho with your camera, you will understand how hard it would be for a bird to catch one!

There are other somewhat bright butterflies, but in the rainforests from Central America down through the Amazon it is always a special treat to see a Blue Morpho!

Here is a Blue Morpho eating some over-ripe fruit that had fallen to the forest floor. Were it not for the fact that this is an older butterfly with a torn wing edge (allowing some blue to be seen) it would be invisible:

Or, for a closer look:

Traveling Incognito

Many insects have a competitive advantage because they have adapted to look like something other than an insect – something a bird or lizard wouldn't eat.

Katydids are the master of disguise. Most katydids look like leaves, and this one also has "eye spots" on its wings to confuse potential predators:

And in both tropical and temperate climates, stick insects ("walking sticks") hide in plain sight by looking like a stick.

And the chrysalis phase of many butterflies – when they would be at great risk of being eaten – often does not look like an edible bug but instead more like a dead leaf.

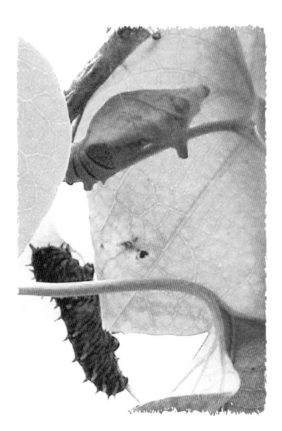

And in what is my favorite adaptation, several butterflies have larval stages (caterpillars) that look just like bird poop! No self-respecting bird would eat that!

Looking Threatening as a Defensive Adaptation

One defensive adaptation is to look threatening to a predator –
even if you are not. This totally harmless beetle has mastered this:

Some bugs and insects look
threatening, and probably are
threatening, but nothing is going to
even attempt to eat them to find
out.

The saddleback caterpillar has several adaptations that help it survive. As with other insects, it has "eye spots" which are large spots which look like eyes, making it appear larger and more threatening. In its case, the two larger eye spots are actually on its rump! It also has poisonous spines.

Many poisonous creatures have distinct *"warning coloration."* Although warning coloration may not prevent an individual animal from being eaten, this adaptation helps give that specie an advantage – the distinct coloration will be remembered by any predator which becomes sick after eating it, and it will not eat another animal like that again.

Other examples of warning coloration: poison-dart frogs secrete a toxic brew in their skin which sickens any predator.

These frogs have long been used by rainforest inhabitants to extract poison to use on darts and arrows so that merely wounding prey such as a monkey will soon render it ill forcing it to fall from its treetop perch.

Some butterflies become poisonous because of what they eat as caterpillars, such as the Monarch in North America and the heliconia butterflies in the tropics.

Mimicry

What if you had not adapted to be poisonous but instead simply adapted to mimic, or look like another poisonous animal? In terms of protecting individuals from being eaten and protecting the species from extinction, this would work almost as well as being poisonous. In North America our Monarch butterflies are poisonous, but not the almost-identical Viceroy and Queen butterflies – and yet they are equally avoided by birds and reptiles. Likewise, there are numerous species of butterflies in the Amazon that look like the poisonous heliconia butterflies.

And not all colorful frogs are poisonous to eat – but they probably do not get eaten very often.

Symbiosis/Mutualism

Symbiosis is when two different species interact in a way which benefits one or both. *Mutualism* is a symbiotic relationship where two or more species work together for their mutual benefit. The existence of bacteria in a cow's gut that break down grass is an example of "mutualism" – both species benefit from this arrangement. These relationships can be pretty interesting. In North America we have ants that "milk" aphids which suck the juices out of plants. The aphids provide food for the ants (whether willingly or not) and the ants in turn protect the aphids from predators.

In the Amazon one species of ant lives within the hollow leaves seen below – the plant provides shelter and food and the ants attack any caterpillars or large animals that attempt to eat the leaves.

This relationship with ants repeats itself with a number of plant species, including some acacia trees. These acacia trees emit an odor attractive to certain species of ants, and a new queen will find a tree to inhabit. These trees contain thorns which are hollow, and in which the ants can nest. The tree also has glands at the base of its leaves which secrete a sugary solution which the ants eat.

In return for food and shelter, the ants aggressively tend the tree – fighting off insects and animals that would eat the leaves, and even destroying young plants that start to grow around the base of the tree.

In the Amazon, the yellow-rumped cacique birds always build their colony of pendulous nests in trees that have certain ants living in the tree. This is because the chicks of the caciques are prone to being attacked by botflies, which lay their eggs on the newly-hatched chicks. The botfly larvae, when they hatch out of their eggs, will proceed to start eating the baby chicks. When the bird colony is next to an ant nest, the ants will comb the birds nest looking for botfly larvae, which are one of their favorite foods! Everyone wins – the ants get food and in return they protect the baby chicks.

In the photo above you can see the large ant nest hanging from the branch among the fairly ragged nests of the black and yellow caciques.

Symbiosis/Commensalism

Sometimes the relationship is one of **commensalism** - where seemingly only one party benefits. Such would be the case when certain species of tree frogs live their entire life far above the forest floor, in the water trapped in the funnel-shaped leaves of bromeliads growing upon branches high in the canopy. These frogs lay their eggs in the pooled water inside the bromeliads, the eggs hatch and the tadpoles live and grow and become frogs never once touching the ground 100 feet below.

I am not sure that this has been studied, but it is possible that the relationship between the tree frog and the bromeliad is actually one of **mutualism** – the frog undoubtedly eats insects, and undoubtedly urinates and defecates in the water inside the bromeliad – this extra bonus of nitrogen might in fact provide this bromeliad with a competitive advantage over others.

Another example of commensalism would be the various wasp orchids that share pollen NOT by offering something such as nectar in return but by fooling a male wasp into thinking that the flower is actually a female wasp! They do this not simply by looking like a female wasp; they have evolved to produce the scent of the female wasp! When the male comes to check out what he thinks is a female wasp, he gets pollen on him which he transfers to the next such flower he visits! In this case the wasp gets nothing from this exchange (except a broken heart!).

Coevolution

Coevolution happens when the evolution of one species forces evolution of another. This is the reason, for example, that specific flowers provide nectar to specific hummingbirds, and specific plants (such as the milkweed) provide food for specific insects (such as the Monarch caterpillar).

This concept was more or less "proven" by Darwin, but not until after his death! He studied the *Angraecum sesquipedale*, an orchid from Madagascar which had a flower with an extremely long (up to 12 inches or more) nectar-containing spur.

There was no known bird or insect that pollinated this orchid, but Darwin surmised that there must in fact be a very large moth with a longer than ever before known proboscis that coevolved with this orchid. There were skeptics aplenty, and Darwin and others even advertised throughout Madagascar offering a reward for anyone finding a moth that fit this description!

This illustration of the unknown moth based on Darwin's theory of the coevolution of the orchid and moth was drawn in 1867 by Thomas William Wood.

In spite of the above drawing and the advertisements seeking this moth, it was not until 1903 – twenty-one years after Darwin's death - that the giant moth responsible for pollinating this orchid was discovered!

This orchid is now often referred to as "Darwin's orchid".

The Leafcutter Ant

The leafcutter ant is a special example of symbiosis. There is nothing quite like it in the world. Leafcutter ants exist in both Central and South America. Leafcutter ants, of which there are 47 species, form one of the largest and most complex societies in the animal kingdom – their underground nests may be as large as 100 feet across and contain 80 million individuals!

The leafcutters above are carrying pieces of leaves into one opening of a very large nest in Costa Rica. Leafcutter ants have different castes with different jobs – harvesters, farmers, soldiers, and workers that do things like clear waste from the nest.

Leafcutter ants harvest pieces of leaves or other plant material which they take back to their nest where it is used to feed a culture of fungus. While the adult ants can eat sap from the harvested leaves, their larvae must eat the cultivated fungus to survive. The ants "farm" this fungus and tend to it very carefully – by preventing other funguses from growing in competition and collecting and feeding it leaves that encourage its growth. These ants actually have a type of bacteria on their bodies that produces chemicals that discourages other bacteria from growing among the cultivated fungus! This is a three-way-symbiosis! And the only place on earth where this fungus species grows is in the leafcutter ant nest!

One night I was walking down a jungle trail with some friends. We were moving in the dark slowly and quietly, hoping to hear some nocturnal mammals such as kinkajou or jaguar. Suddenly we became aware of a sweet flowery fragrance. We turned on a flashlight to look around and could see no plant in bloom. We looked down, and below us was a long column of leafcutter ants marching out of the jungle, crossing the trail, and heading back into the jungle towards their nest. Each ant was carrying a tiny white flower. This small, quiet, aromatic parade was amazing to see and was kind of a magical moment!

When a new leafcutter ant queen decides to leave her nest and start a new colony elsewhere, she must carry with her a "starter culture" of the needed fungus. If she cannot get it started in a new nest and it dies, she will die without ever starting a new colony.

Army Ants

Army ants are not the threat to humans and large animals that people think. They mostly scour the forest floor, cleaning it of dead and decaying animal and plant material. As a swarm of army ants moves through, bugs, frogs, and other animals that had been sitting still jump out of the way. Several species of "ant birds" follow the swarm of army ants to catch and eat the unfortunate creatures that simply wanted to avoid the ants!

This swarm of army ants in the Amazon was about eight feet wide and was moving quickly out of the jungle on one side of the trail and disappearing into the jungle on the other. I had no idea how long the swarm was – it lasted for at least ten minutes as we watched.

Bats!

There are so many bats in the rainforests that they deserve special mention. Bats are the only mammal that has evolved to fly, and bats have adapted to eat bugs, fruit, nectar, fish, and even blood! These very cute white-lined bats spent one day sleeping on the ceiling of my room in Costa Rica.

As evening approached I realized that they all had their eyes open and were watching me. I slowly raised my hand in their direction and in literally the blink of an eye – with no sound at all – they were gone!

In Costa Rica there is also a large bat that uses its sonar to tell when a fish comes to the surface for a bug and WHAM – it hits the water and grabs the fish and flies off for a meal.

In the Amazon these bats found shelter for the day inside an abandoned termite nest on the side of a tree:

The vampire bat is a special case. Vampire bats do not "suck" blood out of a victim. They have very tiny, very sharp teeth, and they bite their prey – often a mammal sleeping the night away. The host may not even stir as the bat sits by or on it licking the blood. Vampire bat saliva contains an anticoagulant – it stops blood from clotting and breaks down blood clots – so that its meal can go on for quite a long time.

The problems with this are twofold: livestock such as cows in areas with vampire bats can become quite anemic (low blood) and weak and will stop growing or stop producing milk. The other problem is that vampire bats can spread rabies.

Vampire bats have a very unique social sharing structure. On any given night only one out of every three or four vampire bats will have success at finding a blood meal. Vampire bats that go more than a few days without eating will weaken and die. Because of this, vampire bats which have been successful, when they return to the colony, will share their meal with other bats through regurgitation.

In an interesting example of useful discoveries from the rainforest, brain scientists now have an experimental drug based on chemicals in vampire bat saliva to use in the treatment of strokes. This drug breaks down the damaging blood clots without harming brain tissue and can allow stroke victims to have a rapid and complete recovery.

Bats are amazingly sensitive to their surroundings as they flit through the night sky. One time on a trip to the island of Tobago, I set out a plate of mashed banana and tomatoes to attract butterflies to photograph. As it got dark I realized that bats were swooping down and grabbing bits of the banana. I got out my telephoto lens and a powerful flash unit and fired away!

Will bats get caught in your hair? Very unlikely – bats have sonar sensitive enough to pick up a mosquito 50 feet away – they certainly are not going to come near your head. However – bats sometimes cannot change directions quickly enough so that if you move suddenly a bat might run into you. They also can be creature of habit – if they are used to flying through an opening to return to their daytime roost and suddenly someone is standing in that opening, it is possible that they might fly into that person.

Arachnophobia!

A fear of spiders (or snakes) is a very good reason NOT to visit the rainforest!

As I lay on my bunk one night in the Amazon, listening to the sound of the rain on the thatched roof and impressed that it was not allowing any water to leak in, I became aware of a very large tarantula on the mosquito net right above my face. I tapped on the net – he jumped and was gone. I was happy, but then I realized that I didn't know where he was…..

It is absolutely true what they say - that in the rainforest you need to shake out your boots in the morning when you get up. Spiders and scorpions may have decided to make a home in them during the night, and when you shove your feet into their brand new home they tend to get a little annoyed…..

Walking through the forest at night with a headlamp is the best way to spot tarantulas as they sit on the trunks of trees waiting for something to eat. You might also encounter a large tail-less whip scorpion searching for a meal.

Or, if you prefer, a good old-fashioned scorpion with a dangerous tail!

There are lots of other interesting arachnids in the rainforest! Funnel web spiders make what looks to be a haphazard nest, but they can lure large insects and even small birds into their nest, where they get entangled long enough to fall victim to the powerful bite of this spider.

There are species of funnel web spiders in Australia that can kill a person with their bite. The ones in the Amazon may only make you wish you were dead!

And this large spider has a problem....

At night, insects that have been captured in its web struggle to get free. Passing bats cannot sense the fine web and think that there is a flying insect there, and swoop down and get the insect - flying through the web and destroying it. The spider has to expend huge amounts of energy rebuilding.

Scientists have discovered that some spiders have evolved to create a thick stripe down the center of their webs. At first they couldn't figure out why these spiders did this – then they realized that the spiders that made webs like this did not suffer from bats flying through their webs! The bats can "see" this with their sonar, and fearing it is a stick or other solid object, will not fly through it!

The case of the tarantula wasp

Tarantulas don't have it easy! They are a favorite food of lots of animals – birds, snakes, lizards – and even a wasp! The tarantula wasp is a mortal enemy of the tarantula, which it paralyzes with a sting, drags off to a small hole in the ground, and leaves it with a deposit of eggs. When the wasp eggs hatch, they have "fresh meat" to eat – the paralyzed but not dead spider.

We watched this drama unfold one day in Costa Rica. The spider defended itself ferociously, but the faster wasp darted in and out and eventually landed a paralyzing sting. After a few minutes, the spider quit moving and the wasp dragged it off.

Above: Tarantula wasp attacking a tarantula in Costa Rica.

The Hoatzin

We have reviewed a lot of evolutionary adaptations that enable various plants and animals to survive in the tropical rainforest. In the Amazon there is a most interesting bird, the hoatzin. The hoatzin is very similar to fossil birds from 46 million years ago, and in fact has some almost prehistoric features. Some claim it could be part of the evolutionary link between reptiles and birds. This is because the young actually have working claws on their wings, which they can use to climb around their nesting tree until their wings develop. The hoatzin hosts bacteria in its crop (an enlargement of the esophagus) which, much like in cows, ferments the leaves that they eat, allowing them to obtain nutrients that would otherwise be unavailable.

The fermentation of leaves within the esophagus of the hoatzin creates a manure-like smell (it is sometimes called a "stink-bird"). This probably offers a competitive advantage – humans won't eat this bird unless they are starving!

It is hard to get close enough to most birds in the rainforest to get good photos.

Paddling quietly at night on a river or lake in the rainforest allows you to quietly and closely observe some roosting birds. This is a pygmy kingfisher seen along the canals at Tortuguero National Park in Costa Rica.

Caimans

Caimans are one of two subfamilies of the family Alligatoridae. The other subfamily is the alligator, of which there are two species, the American alligator and the Chinese alligator. Members of the Alligator family are prehistoric, having survived for over 37 million years. They are aggressive, and generally have few predators except when young and more defenseless. There are five species of caimans in Central and South America, the largest being the black caiman, which can grow up to 13 feet. Currently human hunters (seeking meat and skins) are the major threat to the Caimans of Central and South America.

This is a 12-foot American alligator - up close and personal - in Florida. This is why you don't swim, especially at night, in fresh water in Florida!

Ocean animals in the Amazon?

Some 40 million years ago the western part of the Amazon basin was an ocean. As the land rose, it was cut off from the ocean and became a huge salt-water lake. Eventually it drained eastward towards the Atlantic, but the process of the salt water becoming fresh water took perhaps millions of years. Many animals that were trapped in this inland ocean adapted to the fresh water – and so in the Amazon today you will find animals normally encountered in the ocean, such as stingrays and dolphins! This includes the Amazon Pink River Dolphin. That is quite an adaptation! (Photo by Heinz Plenge with permission)

How have humans adapted to the rainforest?

Humans are recent additions to the Amazon environment, having arrived only about 11,000 years ago. Until modern commerce, humans survived in the Amazon through hunting, fishing, and gathering. Today rural Amazon villages survive on fishing, agriculture, and gathering, with some financial gain through ecotourism. The environment of the Amazon Basin has required adaptation of normal human life, primarily because of the annual flooding.

The annual flooding inundates large areas with water up to 30 feet deeper than during the dry season. Terra firma (dry land that never floods) is often several miles back from the banks of the rivers – in the case above, the Tahuayo River, a tributary several miles upriver from Iquitos, Peru. But the river is life to those living in the Amazon – they could not live miles away from the river. The river systems provide transportation, drinking water, and fish – a large part of their diet.

The result is that they build raised houses on stilts.

During the flood season, to leave your house means taking a canoe – to visit a neighbor, to get food, or to go to the store. The people I met with had small gardens for growing "yucca" (manioc) and cocona (a small plant that bears a fruit rich in Vitamin C), had a few chickens, and frequently ate fish. Purchased rice and beans would round out many meals.

Poor houses consisted of a single room, sometimes closed up, and a separate open house for daytime use. Larger houses had a closed bedroom, an open room with hammocks, and a separate kitchen area.

Above is a yucca field next to a home. Below from the kitchen of another house you can see the "stove" – a wooden table with sand on it upon which a fire can be built. A small table and chairs for eating was present, and you can see yucca and cocona plants next to the house.

And every house has a thatched roof. When you live on $30 to $100 per month, it helps if you can make your own roof! Palm thatch roofs last five years or so. Local inhabitants start making ten-foot long poles of thatch starting a year or so before they will need to replace their roof. They gather flexible green palm leaves in the jungle, and in their free time start making roof pieces. By the time their new roof is needed they can tear off all the old thatch and replace it in a day or two. The thatched roofs are amazingly resistant to leaks!

Above – attaching the palm leaves while they are green and flexible.

The underside of a finished roof:

In the Amazon there are few trails – water is the highway, and everyone paddles! Kids paddle, women paddle, and no one is too old to paddle.

This gentleman was out early one morning catching some fish.

Small wooden canoes like the one above are used when one or two people want to go somewhere close by on one of the tributaries of the Amazon. Larger canoes, often with a small engine mounted on the back are used for family excursions or when goods are being carried to or from the market.

Somewhat larger riverboats ply the major tributaries of the Amazon, ferrying passengers from village to village.

But for travel on the large and treacherous Amazon itself, large riverboats are most often used. The Amazon is a busy highway of boat traffic!

Taking a larger boat out to a sandbar in the middle of the mile-wide Amazon allows you to fully appreciate the river as well:

On a Sunday afternoon in a village on the Tahuayo River, the kids were playing futbol (soccer) and the adults were playing volleyball while the younger kids played in the river (they learn to swim as soon as they learn to walk - or sooner!).

This village is very well off, partly thanks to a nearby tourist lodge that employs most of its staff and guides from the village. Another advantage that I noticed of living where the river floods: in many underdeveloped villages throughout the world where kids run around barefooted intestinal parasites are a huge problem – draining the kid's strength, causing bloated bellies and stomach pain, and contributing to malnutrition. Most of these parasites are spread through cow and pig feces. Because of the flooding in this part of the Amazon, there are very few cows or pigs – and probably a very low rate of parasites.

And they don't miss the cows and pigs. As one guide explained to me, there is always something to eat – anyone can gather fruit in the jungle, and anyone can catch a fish. At one pond in the middle of the jungle he fashioned a fishing pole, found some grubs, and caught three nice fish in ten minutes. Of all the "poor" villages in the world I have visited, the people in this village seemed by far the healthiest and perhaps even the happiest.

As with other pristine natural places, ecotourism helps the local economy and encourages conservation of wild places and wildlife. To visit this part of the upper Amazon, it is possible to arrange accommodations at various lodges near Iquitos, Peru, reached by air from Lima. Generally the staff will pick you up at the airport, transport you to the lodge, provide food and lodging and daily guide service - and they can almost guarantee you the experience of a lifetime! At a number of the lodges the staff speak very good English.

This is the Amazon Research Center Lodge
(www.perujungle.com):

The hammock room at the main lodge:

Medicines from the Rainforest

One important reason to preserve the rainforests is that we continue to make discoveries there that can benefit mankind. The newest rainforest medicine is derived from vampire bat saliva, but the oldest medicine – one that reshaped world history – was brought to the western world from Peru in 1631! Jesuit Priest Agostino Salumbrino observed the Quechua people of Peru using the bark of the cinchona tree to treat fevers. He sent samples back to Rome to see if it was effective against the malaria which was ravaging the Mediterranean area at that time. It was in fact highly effective, and bitter decoctions of the "fever tree" known as quinine have been used ever since. Without quinine water the British Empire would never have been possible.

In fact, Schweppes tonic water containing quinine is the oldest soft drink in the world – going back to 1771! The original medicinal version had more quinine and was more bitter than today's version. The British made the cocktail "gin and tonic" famous when they started mixing in the gin to cut the bitterness of the quinine. Unfortunately, over the past few decades much of the malaria in the world has become resistant to quinine.

(Another plant, *Artemesia annua*, is the basis for one of the newer malaria medicines).

The World Health Organization estimates that 75 percent of the world's people rely on plant medicines for all or part of their medical treatment. This is certainly true in the Amazon.

At the plant medicine market in Iquitos you can find roots, barks, leaves, tinctures, and teas for just about any ailment.

Many vendors offer a huge variety of plant – and animal – material for medicinal uses.

When you travel to see the ruins high in the Andes, the altitude may cause you a lot of problems. Years ago I was walking around the ruins near Cusco shortly after my arrival. An old Quechua gentleman offered to show me around the ruins, and I took him up on his offer. At one point I asked him to slow down because I was suffering from "soroche muy malo." "Soroche" is the Spanish term for altitude sickness. I was having severe headaches due to the 11,300 foot elevation.

He said: "uno momento" and began looking around in the nearby growth. After a minute or two he exclaimed: "Aqui, aqui" (here, here). He showed me a plant, which I later learned is called muño, and demonstrated that I was to crush some leaves in my palm and inhale the minty vapor. I did so – and my headache immediately disappeared! He advised me that this effect would only last a few minutes, but I was happy to wander around for a few days with my pockets stuffed with muño leaves until I had adjusted to the altitude.

With so many plant and animal species that have adapted in so many ways to survive, it is no surprise that we can find chemical compounds in the rainforest that may be helpful to us. The chemicals in the skin of frogs to make them toxic or to protect their thin skin from infection may be the source of our next pain medicines or our next antibiotics. With every species of frog – or any other plant or other animal - that becomes extinct we have lost one more potential life-saving discovery.

This angel trumpet plant contains dozens of biologically active chemicals, some which are currently used as medicines (and some which are poisonous).

Some scientists visit rainforest people and learn from their elders and shamans about which plants they use for what ailments – this is called *"ethnobotany"* and may help us discover new medicines for the future.

Deforestation

In December of 2011 a hurricane swept the southern Philippines island of Mindanao. Hundreds were killed – but not by wind or storm surges. They were killed by flash floods and mudslides which were the direct results of the previous destruction of the surrounding forests.

Mindanao, above, used to be entirely covered by rainforest. Due to excessive harvesting of the tropical wood, this large island is now almost devoid of forest. Mudslides and flooding are now common.

Forests around the world are succumbing to pressures to log. In 1998 the dense forest one mile north of my home in Maine looked like this from space (Images courtesy of Google earth):

Today it looks like:

In Maine the softwood trees are cut for pulp for the paper industry and the hardwood trees are ground up to make pellets to burn for heat and for electrical generation. More than ever before vast areas of forests are being harvested as the value of this wood pulp has increased. The arguments for aggressive logging here are the same as those the world over: we need the jobs and we need the wood (to sell or for energy (or fuel). Wood is in fact a renewable resource, but only when carefully managed and with aggressive replanting of forests.

Poor people the world over are cutting down forests in order to grow food. This is especially sad because rainforest soils are of such poor quality that sometimes only one or two seasons of growth are possible without expensive soil additions. This mountainside in Guatemala, now farmland, was once rainforest:

In Guatemala the deforestation is worsened by the need for wood for cooking fuel and in the highlands, to heat their homes.

In the Amazon, deforestation has proceeded at an alarming rate. U.S. Government data indicates that in 2001 over 60 million hectares was deforested in Brazil alone – that is equal to 230,000 square miles! This land was largely cleared for the production of food, and more importantly, for the production of soybeans which are sold on the world market mainly as feed for cattle, pigs, and chickens to satisfy the growing demand for meat around the world. Brazil is now the world's leading exporter of soybeans. Something to think about next time you eat a burger...

(USDA file Photo)

What can you do to protect rainforests?

1. **Live in a way that doesn't hurt the environment** – for example, don't buy tropical woods. These are most often used for flooring or furniture. Mahogany, teak, and others are very common. Instead look for American woods such as oak, cherry, walnut, ash, and beech. Beautiful floors are now available made from bamboo – this is actually a fast-growing grass that is more environmentally friendly than cutting down huge old-growth trees.

2. **Eat less meat!** So much meat is produced now in large feed lots - "CAFO's" – Concentrated Animal Feeding Operations – that the requirement for feed around the world has forced large swaths of the Amazon to be turned into fields to grow soybeans for export.

3. **Learn about the rainforest** – as you are doing – and share your knowledge and concerns with others. Pass along this book!

4. **Support companies that are acting in ways to protect the rainforests.** Don't hesitate to ask your local lumberyard where their tropical wood comes from – ask if theirs is certified by the "Forest Stewardship Council" (FSC), an organization that certifies that wood is from responsibly managed forests.

5. **Use FSC certified paper** – see if your school district is using FSC paper. A list of paper brands is available online at the FSC website.

6. **Support the formation of parks and preserves** in forest habitat at home and abroad.

7. **Support and donate to organizations that purchase large tracts of rainforest land for preservation** – most notable are the World Wildlife Fund and The Nature Conservancy. Have a rainforest fund-raiser!

8. **BUY some rainforest land for preservation** – you can do this through the World Land Trust.

9. **Support the people who live in the rainforests** in their efforts to save their environment. This can be done through purchasing crafts from rainforest inhabitants and from visiting rainforests yourself. Ecotourism supports efforts to preserve these wild areas. Countries like Peru and Costa Rica are very aware of the value of their rainforests in sustaining the tourism sector of their economy. Learn about and buy "fair trade" products.

10. Support international programs that provide **family planning assistance** to poor rural families to help slow the dramatically expanding global population.

Online Resources:

World Land Trust: http://www.worldlandtrust.org
Forest Stewardship Council: http://fscus.org
FSC certified paper: http://fscus.org/paper/
World Wildlife Fund: http://www.worldwildlife.org
Nature Conservancy: http://www.nature.org
Natural Resources Defense Council: http://www.nrdc.org

Rainforest Education Project:
    http://www.rainforesteducation.com
        (Supported from the sale of this book – provides low-cost and free educational materials to teachers around the world.)

13254697R00043

Made in the USA
Charleston, SC
26 June 2012